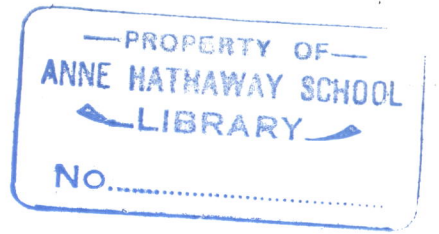

TRACK ATHLETICS

Nick Dean

Wayland

WORLD OF SPORT

American Football   **Judo**

Basketball   **Rugby**

Cricket   **Soccer**

Field athletics   **Swimming and diving**

Fishing   **Tennis**

Gymnastics   **Track athletics**

Editor: Tim Byrne
Designed by RT Partners

Cover: Carl Lewis (USA)
winner of Olympic gold medals
and World Championships at
100m, 200m, 4 × 100m Relay
and Long Jump

First published in 1988 by
Wayland (Publishers) Ltd
61 Western Road, Hove
East Sussex BN3 1JD, England

© Copyright 1988
Wayland (Publishers) Ltd

Picture acknowledgements:
All pictures supplied by
ALL SPORT (UK) LTD.
(except 37b, BBC Hulton)
Artwork by R T Partners,
except 50 by Peter Parr

British Library Cataloguing
in Publication Data
Dean, Nick
    Track athletics.—(World of sport).
    1. Track athletics—Juvenile literature
    I. Title   II. Series
    796.4′26   GV1060.5

ISBN 1–85210–317–5

Typeset by
DP Press Ltd, Sevenoaks, Kent

Printed and bound in Italy
by Sagdos

Contents

This book can be used with WORLD OF SPORT: Field athletics

History of track athletics

A running race is probably the most basic form of competition, and it is this simplicity that appeals to so many people. All over the world people love seeing runners pit their wits and strength against each other as they battle it out on the track. Some people enjoy athletics from the comfort of an armchair while others enjoy actually getting out and testing themselves against other athletes. Over two billion people can be expected to watch the Olympic Games held every four years. This remarkable figure is a far cry from the first Olympic Games which were held in Greece in 776 BC.

The ruins of the site of the first ancient Olympic Games at Olympia, Greece. The ancient Olympics were held for over a thousand years before they were stopped in AD 394 by Emperor Theodorus.

The first Olympic Games

The first Olympic Games were held at Olympia in Greece which is where the Games got their name from. Archaeological evidence suggests that an athletic competition of some kind took place as early as the thirteenth century BC. According to these records the first Olympic champion was a man called Coroibos who came from Elis, who won the sprint race. In fact there was only one race at these Olympics and for his victory Coroibos won a simple olive wreath.

Only athletes of pure Greek descent were allowed to compete at the Olympic Games and victors, such as Coroibos, were treated as heroes. Unfortunately, this pursuit of glory got out of hand, and by the sixth century some towns had set up special training camps for their athletes!

The monopoly of the Games by the Greeks ended with the Roman invasion in the second century BC. It was feared that the Romans would put an end to the Games, but they allowed them to continue provided that athletes from other countries were allowed to compete. Under this new rule, athletes from all over the Roman Empire made their way to Olympia every four years to compete. In AD67 the Roman Emperor Nero competed in the chariot race. He won the event, but this was probably due more to the other charioteers wanting to live, rather than to any great skill on behalf of the Emperor!

The Olympic stadium at Seoul, South Korea, home to the 24th modern Olympic Games in 1988.

Surprisingly, the opening up of the Olympic Games to all nations did not increase their popularity: instead, their popularity declined. Eventually, in AD394, Emperor Theodorus issued a decree from Milan that the 293rd Olympic Games would be the last. After nearly twelve centuries of competition, the Olympic Games had come to an end.

After this period there were few, if any, organized athletic events for many centuries. In Britain, races over both long and short distances were held at village fêtes. Many travelling fairs included strong man contests and other tests of physical strength. Some villages held annual races to the top of local hills and back. These were early versions of today's fell races which are still held all over the country. In the seventeenth century races between footmen were popular along the tow-paths of England, and large amounts of money could be won or lost.

In Scotland the Highland Games were the focus for the country's top athletes. Although running races are still held at the Highland Games, they always take second place to the strength contests such as tossing the caber.

In America the Indians held good runners in high esteem and staged long distance races that sometimes lasted for days. In fact the Indians, with their all-round talents of horse riding, archery, hunting and running must have been some of the greatest athletes the world has ever seen. One Indian,

Wa-Tho-Huck, is considered by many to have been the greatest sportsman of all time. Wa-Tho-Huck was the great-grandson of Black Hawk, the chief of the Sac and Fox Indians and was known by most people as Jim Thorpe. He got this name from his grandmother who married an Irish settler.

He was a superb college American football player and an excellent baseball player. At the 1912 Olympics in Stockholm, Thorpe won the pentathlon easily and then won the decathlon by 700 points. Thorpe was later stripped of his Olympic medals when it was discovered he'd once been paid a small sum of money for playing college baseball. Jim Thorpe may have lost his medals, but he has remained a legend ever since.

Although informal running races existed, there was no real organization until 1812 when the military academy at Sandhurst in England organized an annual sports day. The public schools soon adopted this idea which spread to other schools around the country. Sports days then spread to American schools and by the turn of this century track athletics had become a popular sport.

Growth of organization

Despite the growth in popularity around the world, athletics in Britain was greatly affected by the class system. The Amateur Athletic Club (AAC) was formed in 1866 but competitors in its championships were divided into professionals, gentleman amateurs and amateurs. However, all this ended in 1880 when the Oxford and Cambridge Universities founded the Amateur Athletic Association (AAA). In doing so, they established athletics as an amateur sport for people of all classes.

The founding of the modern Olympic Games in 1896 by a Frenchman, Baron Pierre de Coubertin, provided a focal point for all this activity, and did more than anything to establish athletics at an international level. The first Olympic Games were held in Athens in recognition of the Games' origins and proved a great success despite a poor turnout of athletes.

As athletics began to establish itself worldwide it became obvious that an organization was needed to coordinate competitions and standardize rules. On 17 July 1912 a meeting was held in Sweden between representatives from

Jim Thorpe (USA), winner of the decathlon at the 1912 Stockholm Olympics. The King of Sweden told Jim Thorpe 'Sir, you are the world's greatest athlete.'

Baron Pierre de Coubertin, founder of the modern Olympic Games in 1896.

seventeen countries. As a result the International Amateur Athletics Federation (IAAF) was formed. The IAAF still presides over world athletics and has been subdivided into six committees to look after each area of the world – Africa, Asia, Europe, North and Central America, South America and Oceania.

Thanks to the efficiency of the various associations, athletics has greatly increased in popularity and has become a truly international sport. By the 1930s the Americans had established themselves as the world's leaders and, in a remarkable display at the 1936 Olympic Games in Berlin, proved that sport can be used to overcome prejudice. There is a marvellous story from these Games that sums up the spirit of the Olympic Games.

Lutz Long was the pride of the German athletics team, and Adolf Hitler, the German Chancellor, was expecting him to beat the black US athlete Jesse Owens. He thought this would prove his theory that Aryans (white/non-Jewish people) were the supreme race. In the qualifying rounds of the long jump Owens was having trouble, while Long had already secured a place in the final with a superb first jump. Jesse Owens was looking upset and, with only one jump left, seemed sure to fail. Instead of ignoring Owens, Lutz Long went up to him, calmed him down and offered him some advice. Owens then went and qualified with his last jump.

In the final both men broke the world record, but Owens had the longest jump and won the gold medal. Long then took Owen's arm and led him on a lap of victory around the track to the applause of the German crowd. Hitler left the stadium in disgust.

Jesse Owens (USA) the outstanding athlete of the 1936 Berlin Olympics.

Berlin 1936. The Olympic flame arrives in the stadium to the salute of Hitler and his staff. Hitler used the Berlin Olympics to glorify his Nazi regime.

Athletics today

Anyone who has seen a major athletics meeting will know how much athletics has developed. Highly-trained athletes in bright designer tracksuits jog around the red, rubber track; electronic scoreboards and wind gauges are dotted around the stadium, advertizing hoardings are seen everywhere and loudspeakers announce the names of the winners and play victory music. All this is a far cry from the early, rather stark stadiums that athletes competed in at the turn of the century.

Perhaps the most noticeable improvement for athletes has been in the quality of the clothes and equipment they use. Their vests, tracksuits and shorts are much better cut and made of far more suitable, lightweight materials than the clothes of only twenty years ago. Shoe manufacturers have spent millions of pounds in research to produce high-quality, specialist shoes for training and competition in each event.

Not only has clothing improved, but the equipment used by athletes has also improved. Although most of these improvements have been in the area of field athletics, there are some exclusive to track athletics.

The track

Up until the 1960s most races were run on a cinders track, although Australia and New Zealand retained a preference for grass tracks. All this was to change with the advent of the all-weather track. The first ever rubber-based track was laid in New York in 1950 but was considered to be more of a novelty than a serious alternative to the cinders track. However, its design was improved by an American, William McKnight, and the first 'Tartan' track was developed and laid in 1964. Since then a number of similar surfaces have been developed – Chevron, Mondo, Polytrack, Resisport, for example – but they all share the same advantages:

- They are weather resistant and so last longer in a better condition.
- They provide a spongier surface which helps athletic performance.

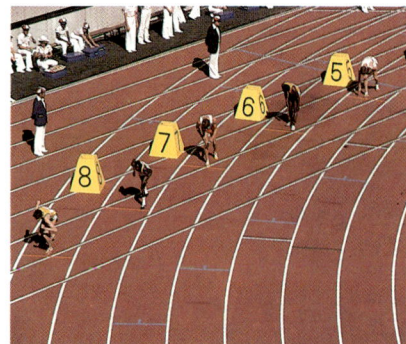

Athletic tracks need to be weather resistant and hard wearing. In this race the start is staggered on the curve of the track.

- The track is less tiring on the legs as it offers a slight cushioning effect.
- The development of the synthetic track has meant that similar conditions can be reproduced indoors.

The indoor athletics track at Houston Astrodome, USA. Indoor tracks mean that athletic meetings can be held all year round, whatever the weather is like outside.

Indoor athletics

Although synthetic tracks suitable for indoor competition did not appear until the 1960s, indoor tracks made of wooden boards had existed for a long time. The first major indoor competition was held in London in 1863 and consisted of the 100 yds, 220 yds, 440 yds, 880 yds and the triple jump.

The world's first indoor championship was held at Madison Square Garden, USA, in 1906 and has continued to the present day. All the early championships were for men only, but in 1935 England became the first European country to hold national indoor championships for men and women. The first European Indoor Championships were held in 1970 and in 1987 the first World Indoor Championships took place at the Houston Astrodome in the USA.

Many of the world's top athletes do not compete in these major championships as they feel it would seriously affect their winter training schedules. However, the standard of competition is consistently high and has proved a major stepping-stone for many up-and-coming athletes.

Top athletes, like the members of the successful US 4 × 100 m women's relay team, can earn a lot of money from athletics. This money is put in a trust fund and apart from meeting training costs it is only released to athletes when they retire.

Trust funds

All of these events are televised and broadcast around the world. With the growth of television coverage came the growth of 'incentives' or backhand payments, to athletes to attend major athletic meetings. This practice became so widespread, along with sponsorship payments, that the line between amateur and professional athletes became very blurred. The word 'shamateurism' was used to describe the situation.

To cope with this situation, and to allow Western athletes to compete fairly with full-time Eastern bloc 'amateurs,' the IAAF decided to take action. In 1982 they agreed to set up trust funds for athletes which allow them to be paid by sponsors. One year later they agreed to appearance money being paid to athletes, but only at meetings specified by the IAAF.

These trust funds have proved to be both popular and successful and will undoubtedly survive well into the future provided they don't break the rule which states:

'Monies accruing from sponsorship . . . are deposited in the athlete's trust fund (minus 15% which goes to the national governing body as a handling fee). Athletes can draw from the trust fund to pay for coaching, travelling expenses etc and will receive the balance remaining in their fund when their careers come to an end'.

Despite their advantages, trust funds have also received criticism. Some people believe that the financial incentives they offer will lead to an increase in drug abuse, a practice which became rife in the 1970s, as athletes strive for success.

Drugs

Anabolic steroids are the most common drugs taken by athletes. They can increase bulk and power, but can also cause liver and heart disease. Other drugs include stimulants to put an athlete on a 'high' and sedatives to calm an athlete down. Despite more sophisticated drug-testing techniques many athletes avoid detection by missing events where they know they will be tested, or by coming off the drug in time to give a negative reading.

In 1986 the IOC tested athletes from seventeen countries, including Russia and the USA, and reported that 623 athletes had failed drugs tests. However, these results are so politically sensitive that the IOC are reluctant to ban athletes. So far all athletes that have been banned for taking drugs have been reinstated. This situation cannot be allowed to continue as it is clearly nothing short of cheating, and if cheating is seen to pay, then the decline of athletics seems inevitable.

Another sad development has been the intervention of politics in athletics. Both the 1980 Olympic Games in Moscow and the 1984 Olympic Games in Los Angeles were affected by political boycotts. It is a great shame that athletes who have dedicated their lives to training for an Olympic gold medal, can have their chances snatched away from them by the politicians of their country.

Ingrid Kristiansen (Norway) with her coach. The relationship between athletes and their coaches is very important. Athletes look to coaches for guidance and inspiration.

However, athletes continue to train and may use today's technology to help them reach their physical peak. Millions of dollars are spent every year to discover the best training techniques. Athletes are wired up, filmed, plotted and recorded to discover the slighest flaw in their running style. Their weaknesses are then worked on by their coaches to produce an athlete at the peak of their fitness on the day of the major competitions.

Like it or not, the 'professional' athlete is with us, and, with the large sums of money they can earn and the international fame they can gain, they look set to remain with us for a very long time.

Clothes and equipment

Traditionally, athletes have worn as little as possible when competing since any clothing may restrict their movements. The early Greek runners solved this problem by running naked! Today's athletes do not have to resort to such extreme measures thanks to the quality of the clothing available to them. Apart from the basic running kit, an athlete must also have clothes in which to train. The most important item of clothing for warming-up and training is the tracksuit.

Tracksuits

Tracksuits are basically the same for men and women. They consist of a loose fitting top and trousers and are usually made of a warm 'breathable' material such as cotton. In the last twenty years new synthetic materials have appeared which are waterproof, hardwearing and allow air to circulate freely around the body.

It is important to wear a tracksuit while you warm-up and to take it off just before competing. You should not work your muscles hard without proper limbering-up exercises – a tracksuit will retain the warmth generated by these exercises and will help to keep your muscles supple until the start of the race.

If it is raining you should wear a waterproof top and trousers. There is nothing more depressing than running around with a wet tracksuit clinging to you. Not only will it restrict your movement, the damp chill will get into your muscles and increase the possibility of pulling a muscle.

For the actual track races, all runners wear a similar outfit consisting of vest, shorts, socks, and spikes or training shoes for warming-up and training.

Vests

Both men and women wear vests made of a lightweight material such as cotton, although women's vests may be cut differently – with a round or V-neck for example. Every club has its own colours which it wears for competition. These may be in plain colours or may consist of stripes or hoops.

Carl Lewis (USA) and Kirk Baptiste (USA) wearing very colourful and fashionable tracksuits. Athletes wear tracksuits while warming-up and training because they keep them warm and keep their muscles flexible.

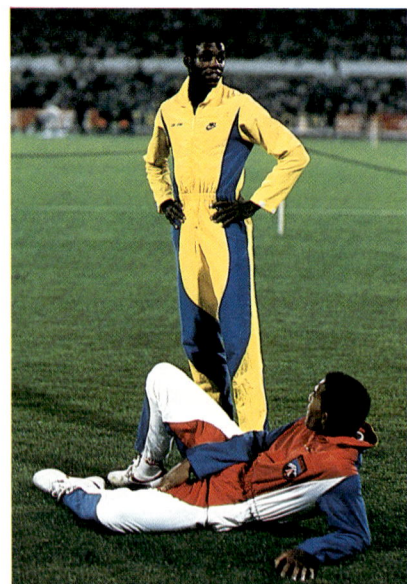

Most athletes wears a cool vest and shorts made of lightweight material like cotton during competitions.

Long-distance runners often wear cotton-mesh vests which allow the air to move freely around the body and so help to keep the runner cool. This is most important in races such as the marathon where athletes can lose up to 6.5 kg in weight through sweating.

Shorts

Again, these are usually made of a lightweight natural fibre but the men's and women's shorts vary slightly. Men's shorts should be lose and cut away down the sides to allow the legs freedom of movement. Women's shorts are usually tight fitting but made of a stretchy material that moves with the body.

Both male and female athletes occasionally wear tights or bodysuits made of the same flexible material. However, these tend to be more popular on the indoor circuits than the outdoor tracks.

Socks

Some athletes wear socks with their shoes and others don't bother. There are no hard and fast rules about which is the right thing to do. If you have a good pair of spikes that provide adequate protection and padding, then you may not need socks. However, you may need them to prevent blisters forming and to provide an extra layer to cushion your feet.

Dennis Mitchell (USA) wears a newly designed body suit made of lightweight lycra. The bodysuit is aerodynamic to allow the minimum amount of drag from the wind which can slow down an athlete.

Training shoes

Today an athlete can choose from a wide range of training shoes that have been adapted for a variety of surfaces and running styles. There are even training shoes to help people with defects in their running style.

Modern, synthetic materials are used in the soles to absorb the shock waves produced when an athlete runs. If there was no padding, the shock would have to be absorbed by the joints in the body which would soon become tired and would eventually become damaged.

Track shoes

Track shoes are made as light as possible but with enough padding to absorb some of the pounding that an athlete's legs must take. An athlete is allowed a maximum of six spikes on the sole of his shoe, but many distance athletes wear only four. All sprinters (that is 100m, 200m and 400m runners) should wear six spikes so that they can grip the track firmly as they power along the track. This is particularly important on wet days, when a thin film of water on the track surface could easily lead to an athlete slipping.

Athletes wear track shoes during a race, with a maximum of six spikes on each sole to help their feet grip the track firmly.

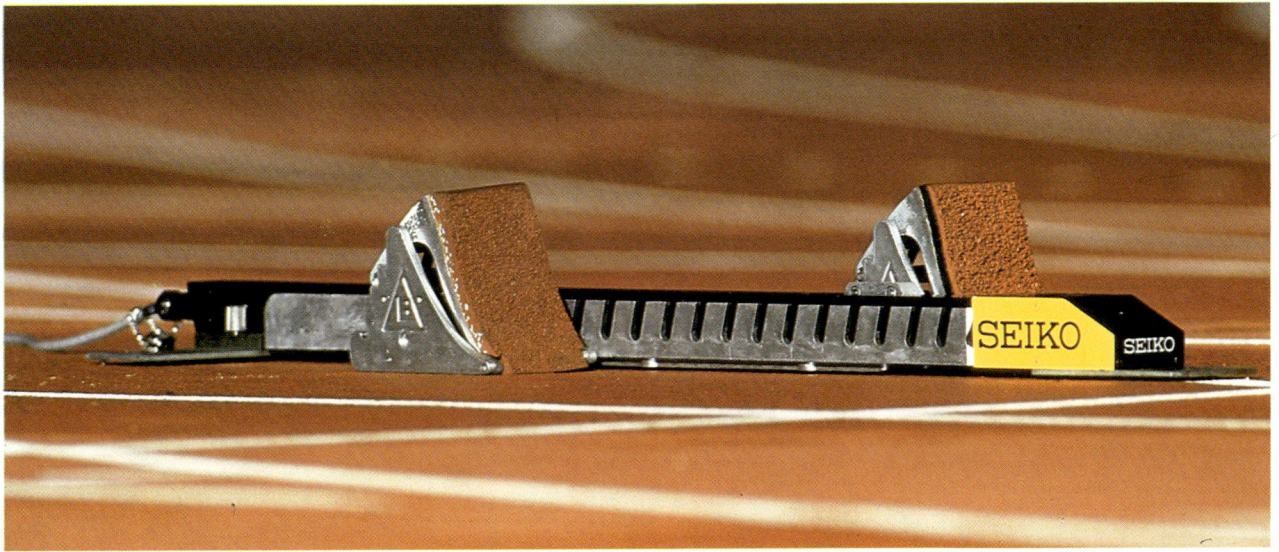

Sprinting blocks

Starting blocks are used by athletes to push off against at the start of a race.

Sprinting blocks of one form or another have been used for centuries. The track at Delphi, in Greece, still has two parallel marble ridges on its track which were used as starting blocks over 2000 years ago. Athletes this century used holes dug in the ground until the 1960s, when starting blocks became more common with the advent of synthetic tracks.

Starting blocks basically consist of two pieces of angled metal mounted on a centre stem which an athlete can push against at the start of a race. The back block is usually set in a nearly vertical position, while the front block is usually set more at an angle of forty-five degrees. The section on page 34 shows you how to set up and use your starting blocks. They come in a variety of styles but all serve the same purpose.

Lane boxes indicate the number of the lane the runner must run from at the start of the race. There are eight lanes on a track. The starting block is positioned at the white line in front of the lane box.

Extras

Sprinters should take along a hammer and two 15cm nails for their blocks if they are to be set on a cinders track; all runners should take a selection of spikes and a spanner in case you should have to change your spikes; safety pins to attach numbers to your vest – the numbers will be handed to you on the day of your race when you check in; linament of some kind and bandages in case you should strain a muscle. Distance runners may also wish to take along a wrist stopwatch to record their lap times.

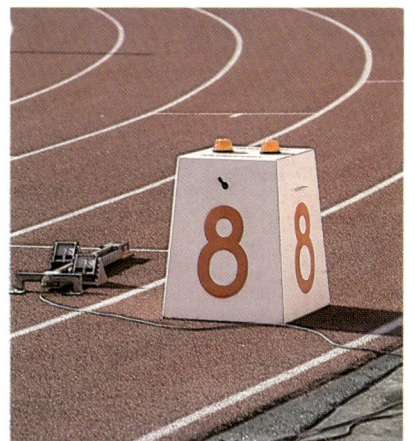

Fitness and training

To succeed in athletics you need to possess the six "s"s. These are – strength, speed, stamina, skill, suppleness and soul.

Strength is the ability to exert force. Athletes must build up strength relative to their own body if they are to make maximum use of their strength.

Speed is the ability of the body to move quickly. In running this is produced by a combination of leg speed and length of stride.

Stamina is the ability of the body to continuously repeat a movement without losing the quality of the movement.

Skill in athletics' terms is the ability of an athlete to 'read' a race and run it to the advantage of his or her strengths.

Suppleness is the range of movement that a limb is capable of achieving.

Soul is also known as 'guts' or determination and is the strength of the will to win.

Every track event requires each of these qualities in varying amounts. Each of the first three "s"s can be developed in a different way for each event. We shall look at these shortly. In the next chapter we shall look at skills and tactics for each event. The two remaining "s"s – suppleness and soul – can be developed in a similar way, no matter which events you try.

Every athlete's training involves physical exercises to make their body more flexible and agile.

Judi Brown King (USA) needs incredible strength and suppleness to leap over hurdles at maximum speed. She can only achieve this through a vigorous training routine.

Suppleness

If you think about the movement of your body whilst running, you will realize that you are continuously stretching and contracting many different muscles at the same time. Your body is like an engine and must be kept tuned so that it can run to its maximum ability. If your muscles are not supple it will be like driving a car in third gear – you can reach high speeds but not the maximum speed that your body is capable of. Your legs will not complete their maximum range of movement and a lot of power will be wasted.

   The following exercises can be used both as a warm-up before your race and also to stretch your muscles and keep them supple.

Warm-up/Suppleness exercises

1 **Jog** gently for five minutes to loosen up.
2 **Neck rolls** – stand upright with your head looking down at your chest. Roll it round in a circle stretching as far as possible to the right, behind and to the left. Repeat in the opposite direction.
3 **Arm swinging** – stand upright and swing your arms freely backwards then forwards.
4 **Hip rolling** – stand with your hands on your hips. Rotate your hips in a circle clockwise, then anti-clockwise.

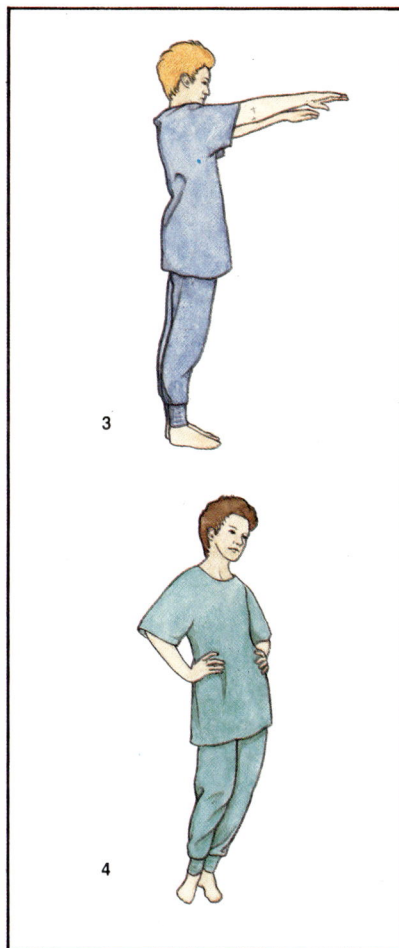

5 Trunk twisting – stand upright with your arms straight out in front of you. Twist your body round to the left and push your arms as far behind as possible. Repeat the exercise on the right hand side.

6 Arm and side stretching – stand upright and slide your left hand down your left thigh, at the same time push your right hand over your head as far as possible. Repeat the exercise on the other side.

7 Alternate leg stretch – stand with your feet a comfortable distance apart. Keeping your legs straight, bend down from the waist and touch your left foot with your right hand. Stand up straight and then touch your right foot with your left hand. Repeat the exercise touching each foot alternately.

8 Touch toes – keeping your legs straight, bend down and touch your toes. See if you can touch the floor with the palms of your hands. Repeat the exercise.

9 Leg and back stretch – lie on your back, with your legs straight. Keeping the palms of your hands on the ground throw your legs backwards over your head and touch the ground. Push your feet as far behind your head as possible. From this position you can bring your legs back in front of you to the . . .

10 Prone stretch position – still lying down with your legs straight, bend forwards from the waist and grasp your ankles or toes if possible. Bob your head forward and try to touch your knees with your head.

11 Thigh stretch – kneel down on the floor supporting your weight with your toes. Lean backwards and, supporting your weight on your hands, gently stretch the muscles on the front of your legs.

12 Leg lunges – sit on the ground with your legs straight out in front of you. Spread your legs as wide as possible. Lean forward and alternately touch each foot with both hands.

13 Calf stretch – stand at arm's length from a solid wall. Keeping your heels on the floor, lean forward and try and touch the wall with your chest. You should feel the bottom of your legs being gently stretched.

14 Bounding – This is an excellent way to finish off a stretching session. Leap as high and as far as you can, driving your front knee hard into the air. Repeat continuously with alternate legs.

6

9

11

13

Soul

Soul is really nothing more than a deep determination to win. Athletics has seen many athletes over the years who have never fulfilled their potential due to lack of determination. It has also seen many courageous athletes, pushing themselves far beyond their natural limits of endurance. In the 1908 London Olympics, Dorando Pietri, an Italian barber, entered the stadium and collapsed several times before eventually being helped across the line. Although disqualified for receiving aid, his determination to finish the race captured the hearts of all who saw him, and he has remained a hero ever since. Although you will never be able to win every race in which you run, however, you should always run your hardest. Provided that you have given a race everything and run your best, or close to your best time, then no one can ask for more. The will to run is undoubtedly stronger in some people than others. One thing is certain though, people who cultivate the need to win, and are able to push themselves harder when it starts to hurt, are those that will make it to the top. Pushing yourself in training can raise your tolerance to pain, but too much tough training can also break your body. Your spirit is often stronger than your body, so be realistic when you are training. Never train when you are ill. Recognize when you are breaking your body down rather than building it up.

In 1908, Dorando Pietri (Italy) collapsed from exhaustion during the marathon at the London Olympics. Through sheer determination he forced himself to get back up again and went on to finish the race.

THE SPRINTS

The sprints used to comprise of the 100m and 200m. However, if we consider Lee Evans' 400m world record run of 43.86 seconds, this breaks down into four consecutive 100m times of under eleven seconds. Even though each 100m after the start is taken at full speed, this is still a remarkable achievement, and shows clearly why the 400m is today considered to be a sprint event.

Strength

If you look at the world's top sprinters you can not help but be impressed by their muscular physique. This is a result of years of hard training both on the track and in the gym. Weights play a vital part in an athlete's training as they can be used in various ways to build up strength and stamina. Sprinters who are trying to build muscle bulk and strength will aim to repeat an exercise about ten times, using very heavy weights. A distance runner will use smaller weights, but repeat the exercise more often – perhaps as often as possible in thirty seconds – this increases both stamina and strength. The following exercises are usually used by

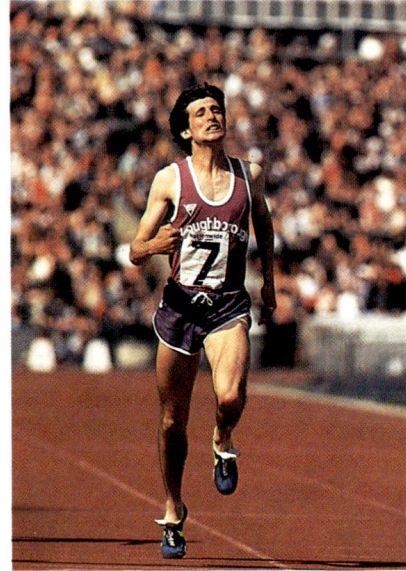

Sebastian Coe (GB) has dedicated years of his life to hard training for the 800m and 1500m.

Lee Evans (USA) ran the 400m at a constant speed at the 1968 Mexico Olympics.

sprinters. If you wish to try these exercises, remember:
- never train without first warming-up.
- never play around with weights; they can be dangerous.
- check the weights are attached **securely** to the bar.
- never weight train alone.
- do not over exert yourself, as this could result in a serious injury.

1 Power cleanse
Stand with your feet under the bar, shoulder-width apart. Grasp the bar with your knuckles facing forward, palms facing down. Keeping your back straight, raise your bottom until the arms are straight. The arms must be fully extended so that the legs start the lift. Pull the bar to the chest in a fast movement. Lower the bar slowly to the floor and repeat.

2 Alternate dumbell press
Hold one dumbell in each hand. Raise them to shoulder level. Push one above your head and then return it to the shoulder. Repeat the exercise with the other arm.

3 Bench press
Lie on your back on a flat bench, with your feet placed firmly on the floor. The bar is taken from a squat rack or handed over by two helpers, and lowered to the chest. Pause fractionally at the chest before pressing it back up until your arms are almost fully extended. The bar should be held with quite a wide grip to improve shoulder mobility.

4 Calf-raising
Hold the bar behind your neck and rest it on your shoulders. You may wish to rest it on a towel. Stand with the front half of your feet on a block about 5cm high. Raise yourself up on your toes so that the ankles are fully flexed.

5 Squats
A great deal of controversy has surrounded squats, since if not done properly, they can seriously damage your knees. Place the bar behind your head and rest it on your shoulders. Keep your legs a comfortable distance apart and bend at the knees. **Do not lower the knees beyond ninety degrees**. It is a good idea to place a chair behind you so that you do not go beyond this level. As soon as you feel your bottom touching the chair, push up again.

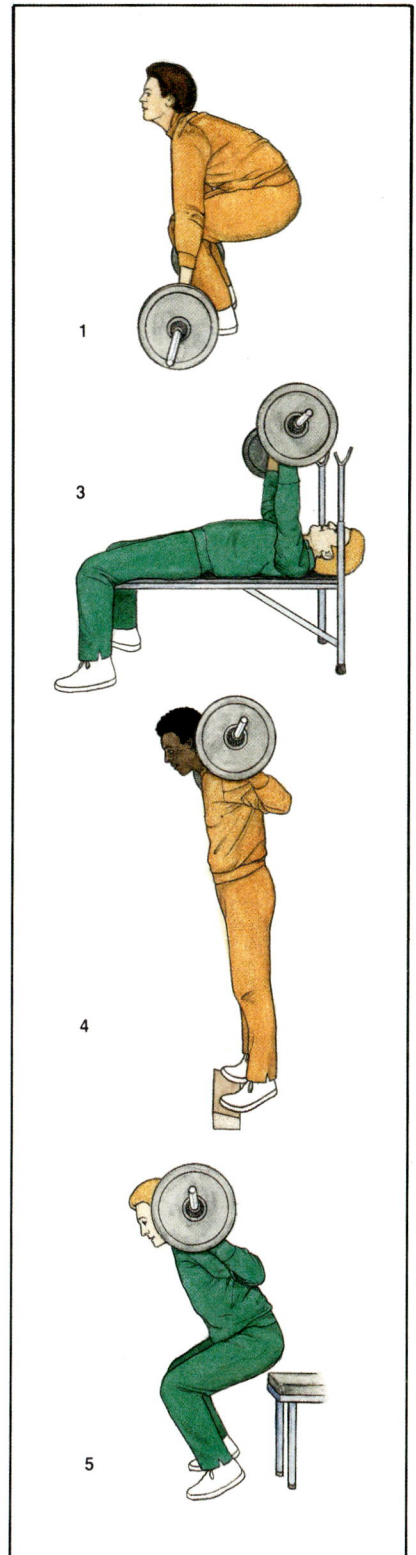

Speed

Speed is obviously the top priority for a sprinter. In the 100m you should be able to maintain your top speed for the course of the race without slowing at any point. In the 200m and 400m you may have to 'coast' for a while before putting in a final burst. Coasting simply means relaxing the body when top speed has been reached whilst maintaining momentum. To achieve this you should relax your arms and shoulders but continue to drive them high and hard. Coasting can only be carried on for about twenty metres without loss of speed, but provides a slight break for the body allowing it to save some energy for a final burst.

The training season is divided into two parts – winter and summer – but it is assumed that the track season takes place in summer. Note which exercises are most useful at which time of the year. The following exercises will prove most useful for sprinters.

Repeat sprints (winter and summer)

This is the most common form of training and should be looked upon as the most important. Basically, you sprint 100m then walk back to the start (or round the bend if you are running on a track) then sprint again. Some coaches believe you should sprint at three-quarters of your full pace, others believe that flat out sprinting is more beneficial. In these sessions you should concentrate on your running style and on relaxing while you run.

Pyramids (winter and summer)

Pyramids are so called because an athlete builds up to a maximum distance and then winds down the other side. For example a 400m men's pyramid would look like this:

```
                400m
        300m            300m
        200m            200m
        100m            100m
```

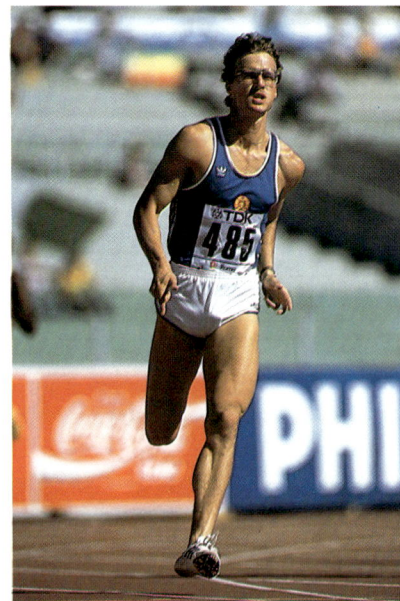

Thomas Schoenlebe (GDR) has trained using the pyramid technique to win gold medals at the 400m.

A 100m/200m sprinters pyramid should be:

$$200m$$
$$150m \qquad 150m$$
$$100m \qquad 100m$$
$$50m \qquad 50m$$

Allow yourself a set time to rest between sprints, two minutes is probably best. As you get fitter, reduce your rest time between sprints.

Winders (winter and summer)

This exceptionally tough form of sprint training is excellent for stamina. During a 400m race, you will reach the point where you are running anaerobically. This means that you are not supplying your body with the oxygen it needs. Some people call this point 'the wall'. Your body does not respond as quickly as it should do – you feel as if you are running in a sea of treacle! Winders will help your body adapt to running anaerobically and keep 'the wall' at bay for a longer period.

Winders consist of springing 150m or 200m flat out, resting for only thirty seconds then sprinting the same distance again before you have recovered. Rest for ten minutes then repeat the exercise. You will not be able to repeat this exercise too many times as it is extremely tiring.

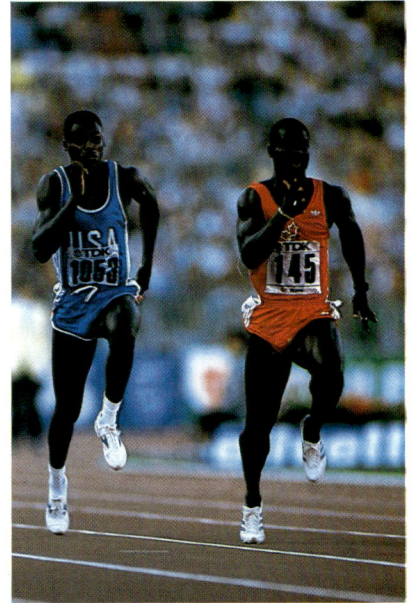

In 1987 Ben Johnson (Canada) beat Carl Lewis (USA) in the 100m. They both trained very hard but the fittest athlete on the day won the race.

Fun exercises (winter)

You can liven up your winter training with a few fun exercises.

Resistance running
Make yourself, or buy, a shoulder harness or a thick belt, and tie it with a length of rope to an old car tyre. Sprint hard dragging the weight behind you.

Hurdle hopping
Lay out eight low hurdles about 1.5m apart and leap over them keeping your feet together. Do two sets of five repetitions over the hurdles.

Hopping races
These can be held over 50m or up flights of steps. If you have steps at the stadium where you train, hop from bottom to top. Walk down and repeat the exercise hopping on the other leg.

Hill sprints (winter)

Find a steep grassy hill, or even better, a steep sand dune. Sprint to the top concentrating on driving hard with your arms and legs. This is an excellent exercise for building up leg and shoulder muscles and developing drive from the rear leg.

Stamina

Stamina does not really play a large part in the preparation of the 100m or 200m sprinter, but is very necessary for the 400m runner. It is impossible even for the world's fittest runners to sprint 400m flat out. To overcome the build up of lactic acid in the legs, or at least keep it at bay for as long as possible, sprinters must develop stamina. The exercises above, especially winders and repeat sprints, where an athlete is sprinting before having fully recovered, will improve stamina enormously.

Olga Bryzgina (USSR) and Petra Mueller (GDR) have developed the stamina needed to win at the 400m.

Steve Ovett (GB) is one of the greatest middle distance runners there has ever been. In 1984 he won an Olympic gold medal at the 800m and between 1977 and 1980 he won 45 consecutive 1500m races.

MIDDLE-DISTANCE

The middle-distance events are the 800m, 1500m and mile. Of all the track events, many people consider these to be the most exciting. Athletes such as Walker, Scott, Coe, Ovett and Cramm have captured the imagination of crowds the world over.

The 800m involves running twice around the track, while the 1500m means running three and three-quarter times around the track. The races are often started from a curved line so that those drawn in the outside lane are not at a disadvantage. At large meetings the first 100m of the 800m is run in lanes; the athletes can then move to the inside lane.

Strength

Middle-distance runners can use weights to improve their strength but there is a danger that they could build up too much muscle bulk. If a middle-distance athlete wishes to use weights he or she should do the same exercises recommended for sprinters, but in a different way. Instead of using heavy weights and repeating the exercise about ten times you should use lighter weights and repeat the exercise as often as possible in thirty seconds.

1 Seated pull-ups

Set up a beam about one metre from the ground. Lie on the floor with your chest below the beam. Using either an under- or over-grasp, pull your chest to the beam, keeping your ankles on the floor. This exercise can be made more difficult by setting the beam higher and lifting your whole body off the floor, keeping the legs at right angles to the body.

2 Step-ups

Use one or two gymnasium benches set to a height of about 70cm. Step on and off the bench as fast as possible, using alternate legs and making sure that you stand fully upright on top of the bench. This exercise can be made more difficult by holding weights such as dumbells or a medicine ball.

3 Sit-ups

Lie on the floor with your hands behind your head. Keeping your legs as straight as possible, sit up and touch your knees with your elbows. When the exercise becomes too easy, try the exercise lying on a sloping bench (with your feet tucked under a rope) or holding a weight behind your neck.

4 Astride jumps

Stand astride a gymnasium bench and leap on to it bringing the feet together, then leap off back to the astride position and repeat. The exercise can be made more difficult by holding dumbells in each hand.

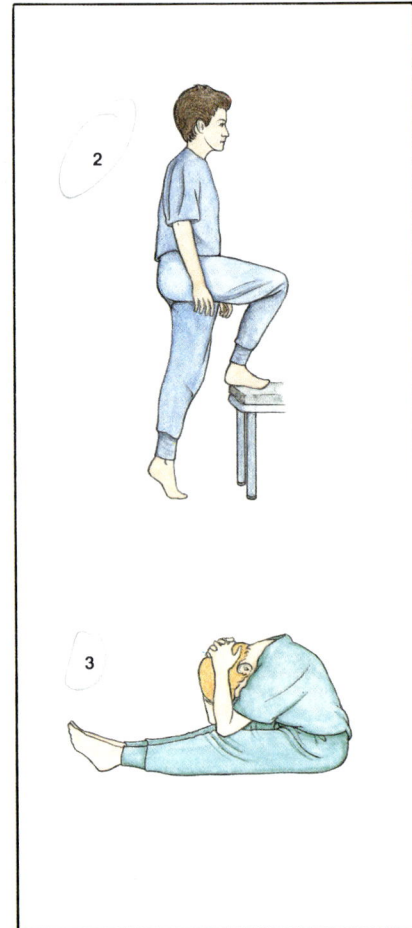

Great rivals Carl Lewis (USA) and Ben Johnson (Canada) are both world record breakers at the 100m.

5 Press-ups

Lie in the front support position and bend the arms so that the chest touches the floor. Push up again to the front support position and make sure the body and legs stay straight throughout.

6 Back exercise

Lie face down on a gymnastics' horse or some stacked benches, with your body from the waist up hanging over the edge, and someone grasping your ankles. Place your hands behind your head and raise your upper body until it is in line with your legs. Lower and repeat.

7 Dips

Place two benches close together and sit down between them. Place your feet and hands on the benches and then push your body up with your arms until they are fully extended. Lower and repeat.

8 Squat thrusts

Lie in the front support position. Pull your knees up to your chest and then extend them again quickly. It is a good idea to mark a line where the feet land when fully extended. Make sure the feet reach the line with each thrust.

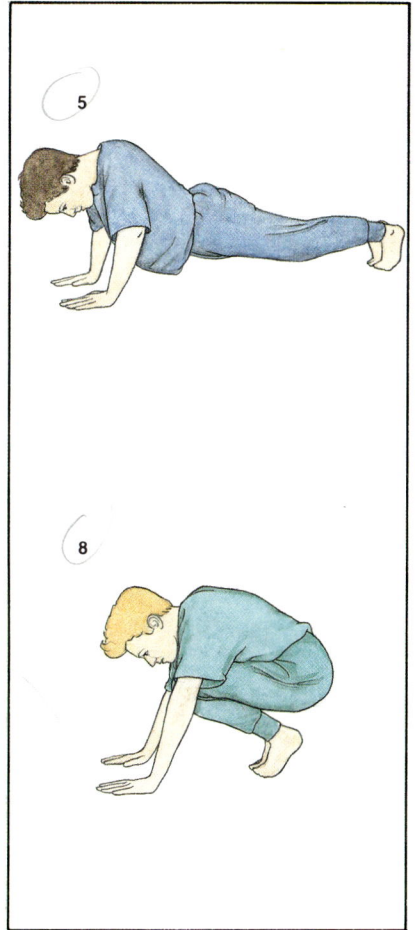

You can see the strong muscles in the legs of these female hurdlers. They have built up their strength by controlled regular exercises.

At the 800m and 1500m Steve Cram (GB) developed and improved his speed technique to become world champion.

Speed

Speed is obviously of great importance to a middle-distance runner as you will see if you watch any top 800m or 1500m race. The 800m often becomes a sprint over the last 200m and those with the basic speed usually come out on top.

The best way of improving your speed is simply by sprinting at full or three-quarters pace over distances between 100m and 200m. Pure sprint work should be saved for the competitive season and used to sharpen an athlete after his or her tough winter's training. The best form of repeat sprints for the middle-distance runner take place over 200m. Sprint hard, but concentrate on relaxing your arms and shoulders and driving your knees hard and high. Walk back to the start and repeat the exercise until you start to lose the quality in your runs. It is then time to stop.

If you are having trouble increasing your speed, then try sprinting down a slight slope of about 100m. The slope will increase your momentum, open up your stride length and help to develop your 'fast-twitch' muscles.

Stamina

This section is perhaps the most depressing for all budding middle-distance runners! Middle-distance races require great reserves of stamina which can only be built up through training sessions that will often be tough and that will test you mentally as well as physically.

Most middle-distance training should be done in the winter, so that a solid stamina base is laid for the athlete to build on. Stamina before speed should always be the rule. This winter training can often be depressing, but is worth it since it will make your summer training that much easier and therefore more enjoyable.

The following exercises should help you to develop your stamina.

Long distance running

This is the most basic form of endurance training and should be done away from the track if possible. When out running –

- Always try and run with friends: it is more fun and you will push yourself harder.
- If you have to run near a road, wear something white or luminous, face the oncoming traffic, stay alert and watch out for traffic.

Work out the maximum distance you think you can run and run it once or twice a week in winter. This will put running strength into your legs for the summer.

Rosa Mota (Portugal) runs through the streets of Rome to victory in the 1987 World Championship marathon race.

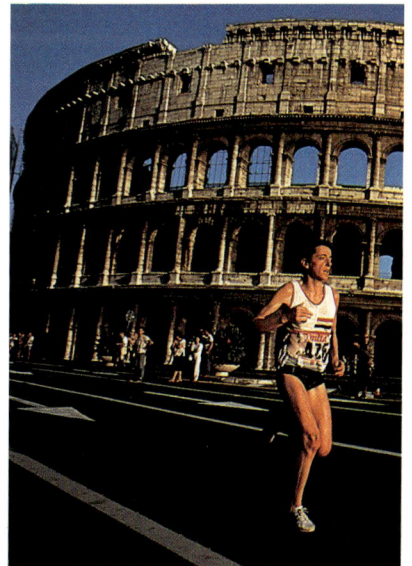

Fartlek

This type of training was invented by a Swedish coach and means 'speed play'. The idea of fartlek is to vary the pace and terrain of the run so making the exercise more enjoyable. For example, you may jog one mile to a hill, sprint up and down the hill six times, walk for five minutes, jog and sprint alternately, jog and then finish with a section of 200m of fast strides with 200m of jogging in-between.

You can plan your own fartlek runs. Some athletes like to jog flat stretches, sprint up hills and walk down hills. Whichever method you choose, remember it is meant to be fun!

Winders

These exercises can be carried out in exactly the same way as described for sprinters, except the distances should be longer.

LONG DISTANCE

Long distance races are generally considered to be those above 1500m. Girls compete in the 3000m–5000m range and boys between 3000m and 10,000m. If competing for a club the IAAF rules state that boys aged thirteen and fourteen may race up to 5000m, boys of fifteen and sixteen up to 6,500m and seventeen upwards can race up to 10,000m.

Training for distance runners is a little more organized as they can use the cross-country season to boost their winter training. This form of racing will not only greatly improve their reserves of strength and stamina, but may help to keep them sharp for the summer track season.

The marathon (42,195m), 10km walk, 20km walk and 50km walk are the longest races of all.

Speed

Although not obviously useful in distance races, speed is actually an essential part of a distance-runners make-up. There are far too many one-pace runners who are quite content to complete lap after lap at a similar pace, but cannot change up a gear for a sudden break or sprint finish.

The great Russian athlete, Vladimir Kuts, showed athletes in the 1950s the importance of speed. He was a brilliant tactical runner who could chop and change the pace from blisteringly fast to relatively slow, and in doing so broke down many of his opponents.

A long-distance runner should do some speed work just prior to the beginning of the racing season and throughout the season itself. Repeat 200m sprints are probably the best or 100m sprints flat out with a walk back to the beginning in-between.

Vladimir Kuts (USSR) was Olympic champion in the 5,000m and the 10,000m at Melbourne in 1956.

Strength

A different kind of strength is needed for long-distance runners. It is a strength and stamina combination. The strength exercises mentioned earlier for the middle-distance runner should prove suitable.

Stamina

This is obviously the top priority for a distance runner and training to improve stamina should take up the majority of his or her training. It is best to divide the year into two: the winter and summer seasons. In the winter a long-distance athlete should compete regularly in cross-country races and put in as many miles as he or she finds possible. Rather than running hundreds of miles a week though, many athletes believe it is better to concentrate more effort into a shorter space of time.

Interval training

This is an excellent way of building up stamina. Work out a course of 12km for example. Run the first 2km steadily, then the next 2km hard, then the next 2km steadily, then hard again. If you are not sure of the distance you are running, then try running steadily for five minutes, then run hard for five minutes and so on for half an hour. You can increase your distance or time spent running, as you get fitter.

HURDLING AND STEEPLECHASE

Areas of track athletics that we have not yet touched on are the hurdles and steeplechase. The high hurdles for men are run over 110m and 400m, and the low hurdles for women are run over 100m and 400m.

The first hurdles were literally sheep fences set into the ground. Obviously any runner hitting one of these at speed would have suffered a serious injury. For years these fences restricted the development of an efficient hurdling technique since the athletes were obviously more concerned with a safe, rather than a speedy, clearance!

By 1900 however, the hurdles had improved enough for an America, Alvin Kraenzlin, to develop a technique of leading with a straight leg which is used by all hurdlers today. Hurdling should not be a sprinting and jumping race, but a continuous sprint over hurdles with minimum deviation from the normal sprinting action. It may take a little while to learn how to hurdle properly, but once mastered, hurdling becomes a fascinating event.

For strength, speed and stamina, the hurdler should follow the exercises suggested for sprinters. These should be combined with sprints over the hurdles and exercises called isolation drills which break the hurdling action down into separate actions.

Walk-overs

This is a very basic exercise where you walk over low hurdles set at 1m to 1.5m spacing. This exercise should remind the athlete of the importance of each stage of hurdling. Remember –

- Pick the lead knee up very high and put it down vertically. It should not reach out in front of the body.
- Keep your hips high.
- Good, wide arm movement to balance yourself.
- Keep your trailing knee in a high position as it is brought through.

Some extra exercises to increase suppleness are also necessary for both hurdling and steeplechasing.

Jon Ridgeon (GB), a top class hurdler, won a silver medal at the 1987 World Championships in Rome.

Suppleness exercises for hurdlers and steeplechasers

1 Ground hurdling

Sit on the ground with your feet on the floor straight out in front of you. Bend your left leg back behind you, so that there is a ninety degree angle between your thighs. Bend forward from your waist and see if you can touch your knee with your chest. Repeat the exercise with the other leg tucked behind you.

2 Splits

Ease yourself down into a split position as far as possible, with your rear foot pointing forward. Use your fingers to balance yourself. Lean forward from the waist and try and touch your shin, just below the knee, with your chin.

3 Hurdle bends

Stand sideways next to a hurdle and rest the inside of your thigh on top of it. Keep the foot turned outward. Bend forward from the waist, keeping the leg on the hurdle, and touch the ground with the hand nearest the hurdle.

4 Leg swinging

Stand sideways next to a hurdle and grasp it with your nearside hand. Swing your left leg loosely backwards and forwards seeing how high you can kick in front and behind.
    Repeat with other leg.

Steeplechase

The steeplechase is for men only and is derived from cross-country events, the water jump being the descendant of the ditch. It is a gruelling middle-distance event run over 1000m (15–17 year-old boys) with eight hurdles and two water-jumps to clear; over 2000m for 17–19 year-old boys (seventeen hurdles and four water jumps) and for men over nineteen, it is run over 3000m.

    A steeplechaser's training should fall half-way between the middle-distance and long-distance runner. It should include extra stamina work, fartlek, cross-country running and some work over hurdles. The steeplechaser should first of all aim for good speeds over the middle-distance events, before building up his stamina and skill using the exercises mentioned above.

Tactics

As mentioned on page 16, tactics, or 'skills', can be included as one of the six "*s*"'s required to achieve success. Olympic medals have been won and lost due to tactical decisions made before and during a race. The following tips may not always help you to win a race, but they will hopefully offer you some options.

100m/200m

As the 100m and 200m are pure speed events there need not be too much discussion about tactics – the obvious tactic is to run flat out from start to finish!

However, it is essential to both these events that the start is achieved quickly and efficiently. Races can be won or lost in the first twenty metres. The most efficient way of starting is the crouch start from a pair of starting blocks.

Setting your blocks

There are no hard and fast rules as to the setting of your blocks, you can only find what's best for you by trial and error. Position the blocks so that when you are 'on your marks', or in the 'set' position, you are comfortable. If you feel cramped in any way, then re-adjust your blocks. The setting will probably be about 42cm behind the line for the front block and 80cm for the rear. The front block should be angled at about sixty degrees while the back should be at about eighty degrees.

'On your marks'
- Walk from behind your blocks to a point a few metres in front, then walk back into your blocks.
- Both feet should be pressed firmly against the blocks, the toes of each foot *must* touch the ground.
- The hands should be placed behind the starting line, shoulder's width apart but with the shoulders leaning slightly over the line. Support your weight with your fingertips.
- Keep the arms almost straight so that the shoulders are kept high.

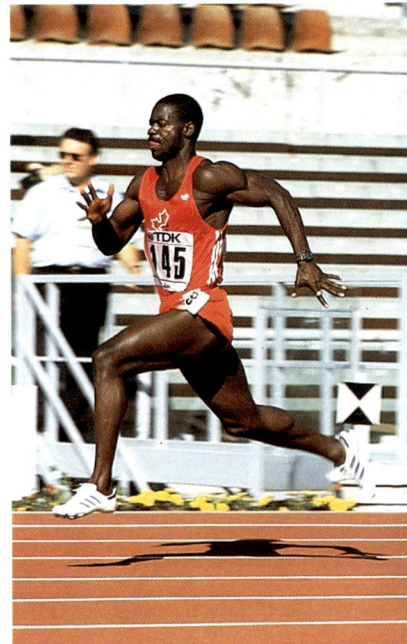

In 1987 Ben Johnson (Canada) ran the 100m in 9.83 secs, faster than anyone had ever run this distance before.

'Set'

- Raise your hips to just above shoulder level and move your weight forward onto your fingertips.
- Move *slowly* into position and look at a point about 40cm down the track.
- Take a deep breath as you move into position and hold it.
- Concentrate on running and driving away from the blocks rather than on the gun.

The gun

- Drive hard and low out of the blocks pumping your arms hard.
- Come out running with long, fast strides keeping your elbows at right-angles.

Once you are into your running, concentrate on keeping a relaxed, fluent stride. Relaxation is especially important in the 200m where there may be some benefit in relaxing (although not losing speed!) halfway down the straight before a final effort over the last part of the race. Too many sprinters actually slow down over the last 20m of the race because they are simply trying too hard and losing their momentum. Carl Lewis, the great American sprinter, claims that his remarkable burst over the last 20m of his 100m race is not him accelerating but the other athletes slowing down due to tension!

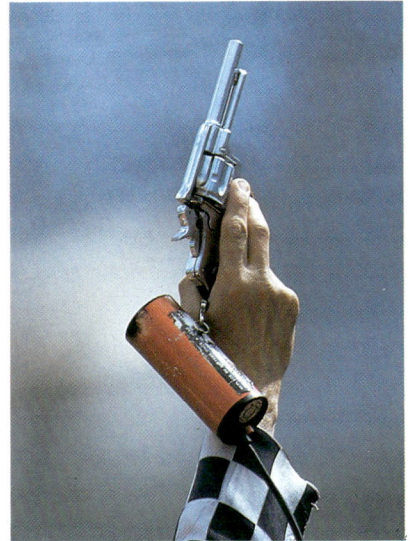

The starting pistol is linked electronically to the automatic time-keeping equipment to make the most accurate timing possible.

Carl Lewis (USA) (nearest the camera) at the start of the 200m. All the athletes start with the maximum burst of speed, yet Carl Lewis claims that it is important to maintain a constant acceleration throughout the whole race.

Seven points for sprinters

- In the 200m place your blocks at an angle so that you run straight into the bend.
- Breathe in on the command 'Set'.
- Run out of your blocks with the maximum possible stride.
- In the 200m stay close to the inside edge of your lane – you don't run as far.
- Relax and concentrate on performing maximum rate and range of leg movement.
- Hold your head up and look straight ahead.
- Run straight through the tape.

400m

The start should be carried out in the same manner as for the 100m and 200m.

- This initial speed should be carried on right round the first bend.
- The initial speed should only be slightly slower than the top speed.
- Fast sprinters should use their speed to bring them into the lead on the home straight. A leading position at this stage can produce reserves of energy you never knew existed!
- Try and keep relaxed the whole way round. Tension in the shoulders can lead to a cramped style and wasted energy.
- Keep to the inside of your lane when running the bends.
- Run through the tape, don't ease up beforehand.

800m

The 800m is considered a middle-distance event but at international level the split times show it to be almost a prolonged sprint. The first 100m is run in lanes so the athletes are staggered at the beginning of the race. They then close to the inside of the track. It is interesting to watch 800m races to see the positions the athletes try to adopt. Ideally, you should be placed on the shoulder of the person in second or third place. In this way you can cover any breaks from the front or back of the pack. Also try to:

- Stay as close to the inside of the track as possible; in this way you run no further than you have to.
- Position yourself on the shoulder of one of the leading runners.

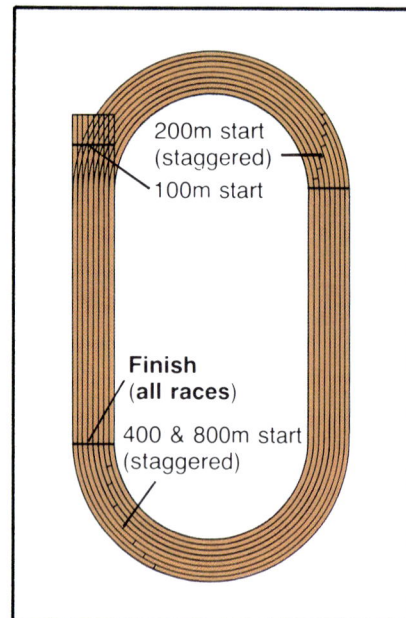

Sprint

Billy Konchellah (Kenya), world 800m champion in 1987, has learnt the techniques needed to be a winning athlete.

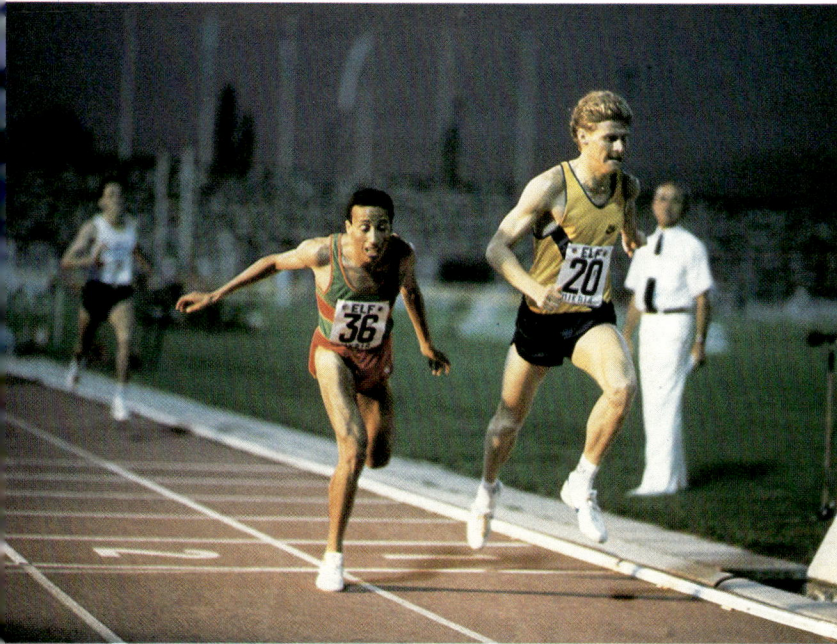

Steve Cram (GB) and Said Aouita, (Morocco) great competitors at the 1500m.

- Pass on the straights wherever possible and when you pass someone, run hard and fast. Be positive.
- In a slow race go for the tape early. In a fast race save your finishing sprint for as long as possible.
- Fight hard all the way to the finish!
- When you start to tie up – relax! Drop your shoulders, keep your fingers loose and drive hard with your arms. If your arms drive hard, your legs must follow.

1500m

The 1500m, or metric mile, probably has more romance surrounding it than any other track event. For years athletes dreamed of breaking the four minute barrier for the mile. Then, on 6 May 1954, at the Iffley Road track in Oxford, Roger Bannister of England became the first man in history to run the mile in under four minutes with a time of 3 minutes, 59.4 seconds.

On the whole, tactics for 1500m should be the same as for the 800m, however, there are a few other points.

- Try to distribute your energy and pace as evenly as possible over the whole race.
- Move up towards the leader between laps two and three.
- If you are leading, run at your pace but start to pick it up after the first two-and-a-half laps.

In 1954 Roger Bannister (GB) became the first person to run the mile in less than 4 minutes. Athletes today can run the metric mile (1500m) in almost 30 seconds faster than Roger Bannister's record.

Distance races (3,000m, 5,000m, 10,000m)

In the long-distance races, fitness rather than tactics is very often the decider at the end of the day. Any athlete who doesn't have the 'pace' in his or her legs simply won't be able to hang on lap after lap in a fast race. Providing you are in good shape, there are various ways of running your race.

- The most economical way to run a distance race is to run at an even pace throughout. This should be your aim as far as possible. To win a race by even pace you should first calculate what you consider to be a winning time, break it down into lap times then run your race falling to within a second of each lap time.
- If you are very fit and psychologically very strong you could try and 'break' the rest of the field. This involves running alternate fast and slow laps and never letting the pace settle. This is certainly the hardest way to run a race, but if successful, by far the most rewarding.
- Positioning is important in a distance event. In the early and middle sections of the race you can allow yourself to stay 20m or even 30m from the front of the pack. This may even be advantageous in a large field where the outside runners at the front of the pack may be forced to run wide round every bend. Towards the end of the race make sure you are in no danger of being 'boxed in' on the inside lane and therefore unable to follow any breaks from the front.
- The burst! Races are rarely won by someone just plodding determinedly around. At some stage a conscious decision must be made to put in an explosive effort and break away from the rest of the pack. This burst can come in the middle of the race, towards the end, or on the last lap – but it must be decisive. Only you can tell how strong you are feeling, and judge how good the opposition is, but once you go, don't look back, pump your arms and keep running!
- Don't just stop after your race. Walk around for a while until your breathing has slowed down then jog for ten minutes or so. This gives your body a chance to 'warm-down' and will help your muscles to relax.

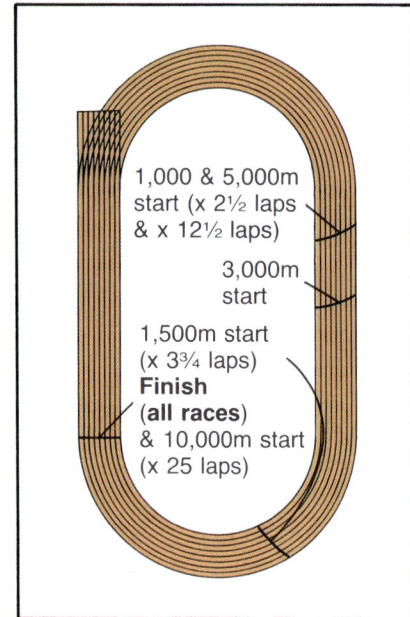

1,000 & 5,000m start (x 2½ laps & x 12½ laps)

3,000m start

1,500m start (x 3¾ laps)
Finish (all races) & 10,000m start (x 25 laps)

Middle distance

(Right) Said Aouita (Morocco) fastest person in the world at the 1500m.

Ingrid Kristiansen (Norway), wearing number 453 on her vest, leads the women's 10,000m race. Long-distance races demand the greatest stamina from athletes.

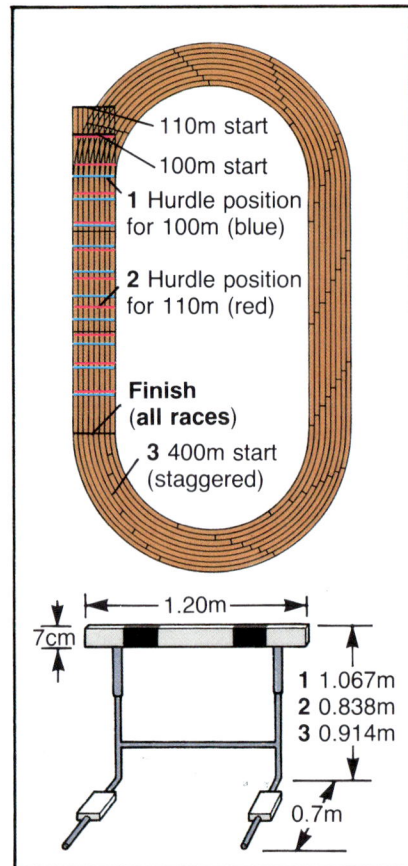

Hurdling

To hurdle well you should really acquire the services of a good coach. Both the 100m and 400m hurdles races require the athlete to clear ten hurdles.

A hurdler should aim to take eight strides to the first hurdle and three strides in between each hurdle.

110m start
100m start
1 Hurdle position for 100m (blue)
2 Hurdle position for 110m (red)
Finish (all races)
3 400m start (staggered)

1.20m
7cm
1 1.067m
2 0.838m
3 0.914m
0.7m

Hurdles

(Top left) This multi-exposure photograph shows the take-off, clearance and land needed to be a successful hurdler.

(left) Hurdling requires extreme concentration as a hurdler views the prospect ahead and prepares for the challenge of a race.

In the 400m hurdles the hurdling technique is not quite as important, so you can afford to clear the hurdles a little higher. This should only be done to gain ground on the other side of the hurdle though. Any time spent over the hurdle is time wasted.

- Attack the hurdle.
- Keeping the rear leg on the ground as long as possible may help you to avoid jumping rather than hurdling.
- Bring the rear leg through quickly and late.
- Use your arms to help your style. As you clear the hurdle pull back the lead arm vigorously and punch the opposite hand forward.
- Get into a smooth rhythm and hold it to the end of the race. Stuttering steps between hurdles will waste a lot of time.

Fractions of a second separate these women as they clear a row of hurdles.

Steeplechase

The steeplechase event is for men only. The standard Olympic steeplechase event is the 3000m. This means the steeplechase runner must run seven-and-a-half laps of the track clearing twenty-eight hurdles and seven water jumps. Unlike the 100m, 110m and 400m hurdles events, the hurdles in steeplechase are very heavy and made of solid wood. This means that a runner can actually tread on the hurdle as he passes over it. In fact only the water jump hurdle should be stepped on; the other hurdles should be clearly jumped.

Francesco Panetta (Italy) is a 3,000m steeplechase champion. Steeplechasers need to clear twenty-eight hurdles and seven water jumps.

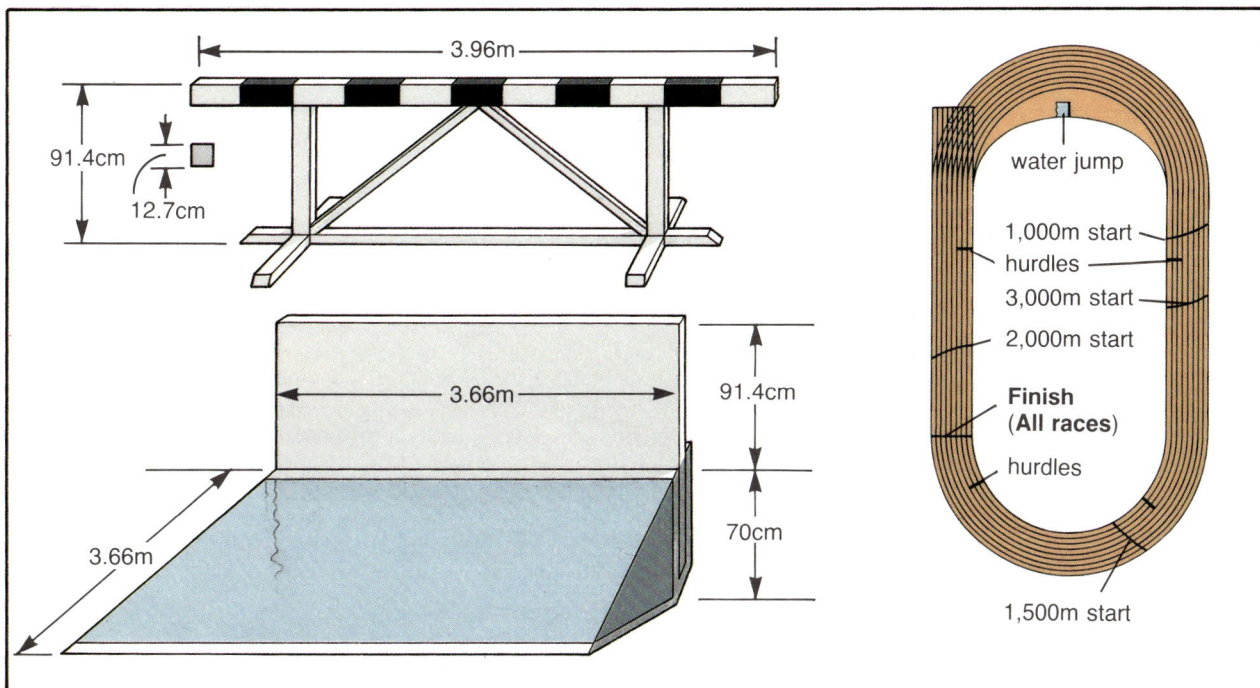

Steeplechase

Take-off for the water jump should take place about 1.50m from the hurdle. Some runners place a marker approximately 15m from the hurdle so that they can pace their run-up to the hurdle. On reaching the hurdle you should drive at it hard with your leading leg and place the ball of your foot on the hurdle rail. In this way your spikes will grip the top of the hurdle – **never try and jump the water hurdle in shoes without spikes as you could seriously injure yourself**. Keep the lead leg slightly bent so that you can push yourself hard to the far end of the water jump. Push long and hard against the hurdle as you jump away from it. Place one foot in the water and bring your trailing leg through high before running hard onto your next stride.

- Settle into a rhythm as soon as possible. Chopping and changing your stride length will not only tire you more quickly, it will also make it more difficult to gauge your approach to the hurdles.
- Hurdle each obstacle as economically as possible.
- Be aware of the runners around you. As the race goes on you are more likely to collide with other athletes as tiredness sets in.
- Attack the hurdles.

Relay racing (4 × 100m & 4 × 400m)

The relay races are usually the final track events of the day and often prove to be the most exciting. There is more to relay racing than simply passing a baton from athlete to athlete at speed. There are a number of factors that need to be considered.

Order of running

The first and third runners have to run the bends, so obviously good bend runners should be put there. Your first runner should also be someone with a reliable fast start.

The second and third runners also have to receive *and* pass the baton so they should have good handling skills. The second runner can also run a longer leg by taking the baton early and handing it over late. If you have a 200m specialist in your team, they should run this leg. The last runner is usually the fastest member of the team as they are the most likely to hold off a challenge or close down on a leading runner.

Setting off

It is essential for a smooth take-over that both the incoming and outgoing athletes are travelling at the same speed when the hand-over takes place. If either is wrong then a collision or a missed baton change may result.

To avoid incidents like these you should place a marker (usually a piece of tape or a splash of talcum powder) on the track about twenty footsteps from the start of the acceleration zone. As soon as the incoming runner hits that mark you should set off as fast as possible. Don't worry about leaving the incoming runner behind, he or she will already be travelling at full speed. The exchange itself should take place in the last third of the zone when the outgoing runner should be reaching full speed. Don't put your hand out for the baton until the incoming runner shouts at you to do so.

Handing over the baton

The baton is usually passed with alternate hands; that is from the left hand to the right hand, then the right hand to the left hand of the first runner. So if you are receiving the baton in your right hand, run slightly more to the left of the lane and get the incoming runner to run to the right hand side of the lane. This will allow the baton to be passed easier.

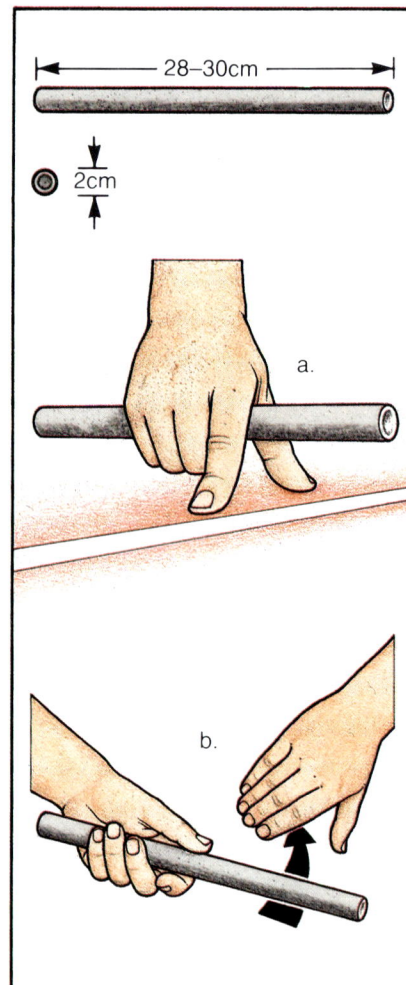

Relay

The baton can be passed using either an upsweep or a downsweep of the arm. Nowadays most athletes use the upward sweep as it is much easier to perform. Any mistakes can be quickly corrected, and the outgoing runner can move off fast and still present a steady hand to the incoming runner. The main difficulty is in placing the baton so that the outgoing runner can obtain a good grip, while leaving enough of the baton free to hand on to the next runner. There are no easy solutions to this problem which must be sorted out in team practise.

The main advantage of the downsweep is that the baton is passed into an upturned palm, which leaves more of it free to pass onto the next person.

4 × 400m relay

The first 500m of the 4 × 400m relay is run in lanes. The runners are then allowed to break to the inside lane. This makes it difficult to plan your hand-overs exactly, as there will be runners all around you, also waiting to receive the baton. You should not set off too soon or too quickly in the 4 × 400m relay as the incoming runner will almost certainly be slowing right down as he or she approaches. Always put your best runner in last in this event.

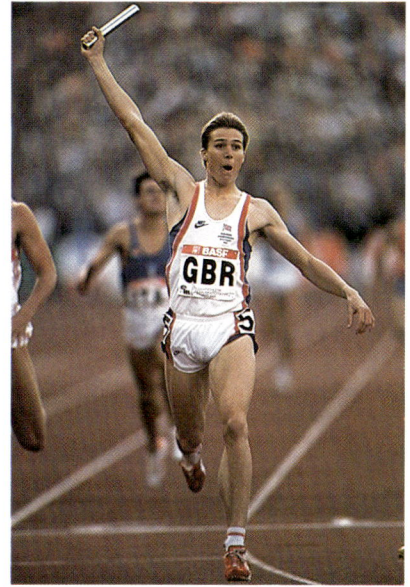

Roger Black (GB) the last member of the 4 × 400m team holds the baton high in victory.

The changeover of the baton needs to be done swiftly. The receiver starts to run before the incoming athlete hands the baton over. The picture shows a women's 4 ×100m race.

Championships

Every year there are dozens of competitions around the world where top athletes can test themselves against each other. However, the world's major championships are the true testing grounds of the world's elite. To win at a major championship such as the Olympic or World Games takes something extra. Every top athlete in the world will have been training for that championship, will have timetabled their training and race schedule to peak at that particular time, and will arrive eager to win, ready to push themselves to the limit. As the great runner Herb Elliott remarked, 'The athlete's life is painstakingly moulded so that for a few seconds, or minutes, on a certain day, he will be able to give his maximum effort'. Anyone who can win a race at this level of competition deserves to be called a champion.

Anyone can participate in athletics. These disabled athletes compete in the wheelchair race at the World Championships in 1987.

The Olympic Games

On 25 November, 1892, a Frenchman, Baron Pierre de Coubertin gave a lecture at the Sorbonne in Paris where he put forward the idea of reviving the Ancient Olympic Games. His speech proved a great success and four years later de Courbertin was hailed as the 'founder of the Modern Olympic Games,' as the first Olympics for 1,503 years were held in Athens, Greece.

An estimated 80,000 spectators watched the nine different sports that made up the first Olympics. The thirteen-man squad from the USA came out on top in the athletics, winning nine out of the twelve track and field events.

Since then the Games have grown considerably with a record number of 122 countries competing in the 1972 Munich Games. Unfortunately some countries have tried to use the Olympics as a showcase for their political views. This led to terrorism in the 1972 Munich Games when eleven members of the Israeli team were killed by Palestinian terrorists, and political boycotts of each other's Games by the USA and Russia in 1980 and 1984. Activities such as these run directly against the original ideal of the Olympic Games, which was to unite athletes of all nations in their aim to achieve personal triumph.

With so much money and prestige at stake in the modern Olympic Games, it would be nice if today's athletes remembered those old ideals and what they stood for. As Baron de Coubertin said at the first Games,

'The important thing in the Olympic Games is not winning but taking part. The essential thing in life is not conquering but fighting well.'

The important message of the Olympics said by Baron de Coubertin at the 1896 Athens Olympics.

THE IMPORTANT THING IN THE OLYMPIC GAMES IS NOT WINNING BUT TAKING PART. THE ESSENTIAL THING IN LIFE IS NOT CONQUERING BUT FIGHTING WELL.
BARON de COUBERTIN

IAAF World Championships

It is remarkable that up until 1983 there were no official world championships for athletics. The IAAF recognized the Olympic Games as being the official world championships so every Olympic champion automatically became the world champion.

All this changed in 1983 when the IAAF organized the first World Championships in Helsinki. The event was a great success and attracted 1,570 of the world's top athletes from over 150 countries. The Championships are now to be held every four years in the year before the Olympic Games.

European Championships

The European Championships came about thanks to the efforts of the Hungarian IAAF representative Szilard Stankovitz. The decision to hold the first European Championships in Turin in 1934 was taken after a meeting

The Rome Olympic stadium is floodlit allowing events to take place after dark. The 1987 World Championships were held in this stadium.

of IAAF members in November, 1932.

The first championships attracted athletes from sixteen European countries excluding Britain and the USSR. At first the women and men competed at separate venues, but in 1946, and ever since, they have competed together.

Open to athletes eligible to represent any European country, the European Championships are held every four years and always produce an exceptionally high standard of competition.

Commonwealth Games

Originally called the British Empire Games, these championships were first held in Hamilton, Canada, in 1930. These first Games were organized by Bobby Robinson, an ex-Canadian team manager and sports reporter for the local paper, *The Hamilton Spectator*.

The organization of the Games was taken over by the British Empire Games Federation in 1932, and in 1934, when the event was held in London, women competed for the first time.

The British Empire Games were renamed the Commonwealth Games in 1970. In 1986 the Games were held in Edinburgh but a number of countries boycotted the event, due to British involvement with South Africa.

Pan American Games

The Pan American Games are held exclusively for athletes from the American continents, North and South.

A forerunner of the present Pan American Games, called the Pan Exposition Games, were held in Dallas in 1937. The present system was due to start in 1942 but was postponed because of American involvement in the Second World War. The first Pan American Games were eventually held in Buenos Aires, Argentina in 1951 and have been held every four years since.

Although these are considered to be the most important athletics championships, there are many others which hold great prestige. The largest of these are: the African Games, the Asian Games, the Balkan Games and the Mediterranean Games. Another one that is fast becoming seen as a major championship is the World Student Games. These are held for athletes in full-time further education.

The moment that athletes dream of is receiving a winners medal. Jon Ridgeon (GB) and Greg Foster (USA) celebrate victory in 110m hurdles.

Venues

Although athletics meetings have never attracted the massive crowds seen at other sports stadiums, the major championships more than compensate for this. At the Olympic Games and World Championships, the athletics stadium is by far the most popular venue, as people from all over the world come to cheer their athletes.

Athletics stadiums vary enormously in appearance, the space-age web of Munich's Olympic Stadium is in complete contrast to the wide-open bowl of the Los Angeles Coliseum for example. However, the venues all measure up to exact international standards and the sites have been carefully selected.

Before building a stadium, it is vital to consider the layout of the track and the land on which it is sited. Poor drainage may lead to difficulties with the track surface, the prevailing wind should always be behind the sprinters on the home

An athletics stadium showing the uses of the track.

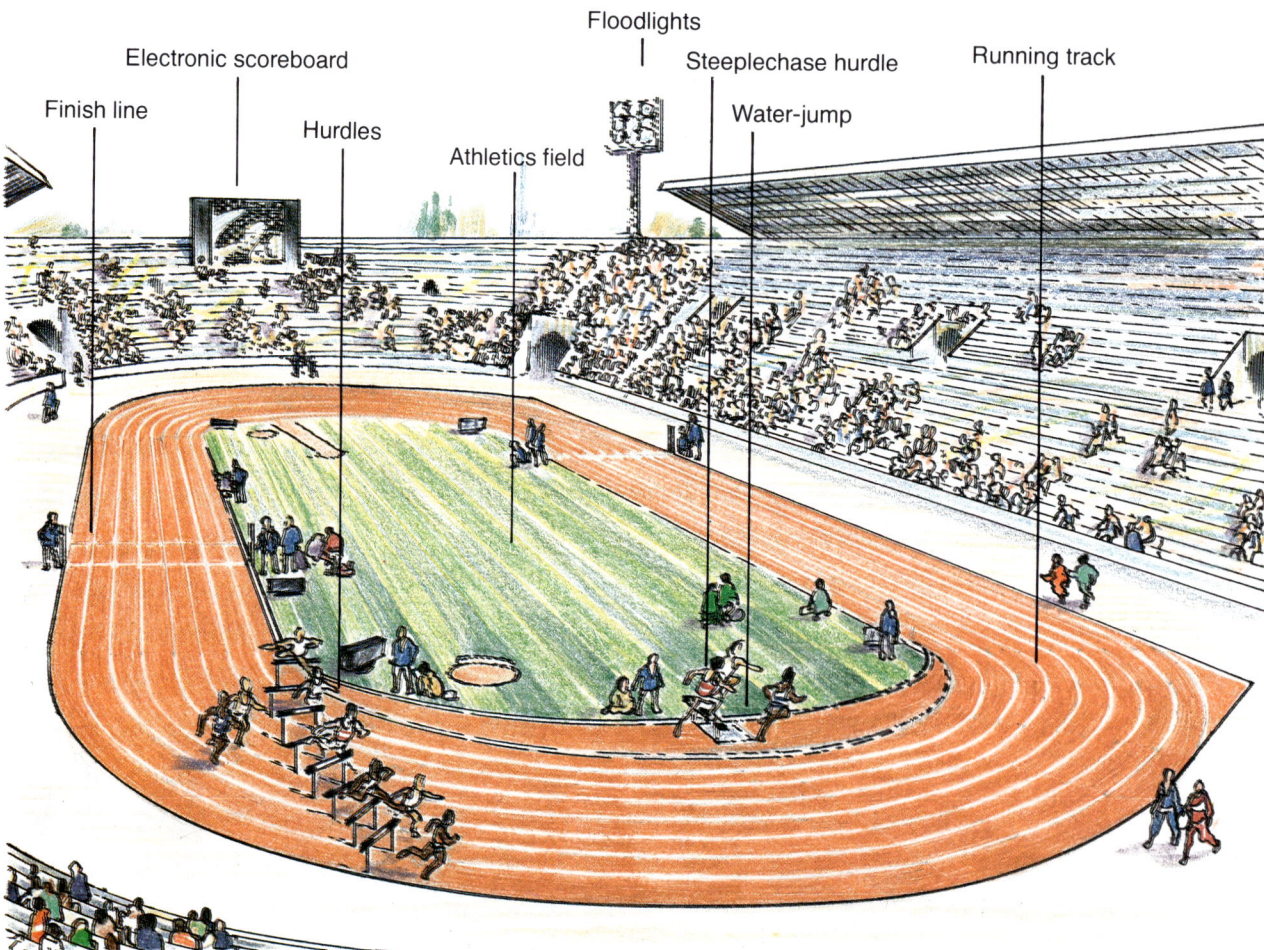

Floodlights

Electronic scoreboard

Steeplechase hurdle

Running track

Finish line

Hurdles

Water-jump

Athletics field

straight, and the position of the afternoon sun should also be considered for the field athletes.

The standard athletics track is a 400m circuit, containing two 80m straights bordered by a kerb on the inside lane. This kerb is important as it marks clearly the inside of the track and ensures that athletes do not put a foot off the track if they pass on the inside. It has, however, caused athletes to fall in the past, adding great drama to many a race.

The track is usually divided into six or eight lanes, although there are a few nine lane stadiums in the world. In the early days, tracks were divided up by ropes slung low between each lane. These proved to be very dangerous, however, as any tired athlete could easily stray slightly and be sent crashing to the floor.

In the 200m and 400m races, the lanes are staggered so that all the athletes run the same distance. Obviously an athlete on the inside lane will have less distance to run than an athlete level with him or her on the outside lane. Many athletes feel it is an advantage to be drawn in one of the middle lanes – a draw on the inside lane means you have to run a tight bend; athletes on the outside lane do not have anyone to run at, and so find it difficult to pace themselves.

All the top championship meetings use electronic timing to record the athletes' times. The electronic timing system is triggered by the starter's gun which is wired up to pressure pads on the athletes' starting blocks. If an athlete's foot leaves the block before the gun has fired (a false start), a red light will appear on the box behind that athlete. This box also houses a small loud speaker so that the starter's orders can be clearly heard by all the athletes.

Starting blocks are used by athletes in the 100m, 200m and 400m. They were first used effectively in 1927 by two Americans, George Bresnahan and William Tuttle. Tests have shown that blocks can improve an athlete's start and nowadays all top athletes use them.

Not only can there be trouble starting the races, there can often be even more difficulty judging the finish! In many races, but especially in the sprints, it is often difficult to decide the outcome of a close race. This problem was solved in the 1940s with the invention of the photofinish camera. Basically, the camera is positioned so that it looks straight across the finish line. As the athletes cross the line, a sequence of photographs are taken from which the positions

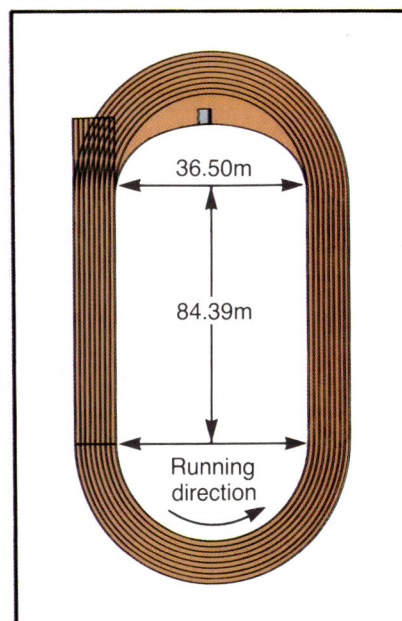

36.50m

84.39m

Running direction

General (dimensions)

can be judged. Modern photofinish cameras are actually more complex than this and produce a strip of film so that the position of each athlete as they cross the line can be decided. Modern film also shows the athlete's times along the bottom of the strip. In this way times can be accurately measured to within one thousandth of a second.

In the sprint and hurdles events up to 200m and the long and triple jumps, a wind gauge is used to measure the speed of the wind. If the wind is blowing stronger than 2m/second, the time is noted as being wind-assisted and cannot be registered as a record.

The wind gauges can be seen halfway down the home straight and 20m from the take-off board in the long and triple jump pits.

Another feature of the modern athletics' stadium is the electronic scoreboard which will flash up lane draws and results. Smaller scoreboards are dotted around the stadium and display field event results and lap times for both the athletes' and the spectator's information.

All of these features can be seen in the world's top athletics arenas, listed below.

Bislett Stadium

Although Norway has produced few great athletes in recent years (barring their javelin throwers and distance runners), they have perhaps the most fanatical supporters in the world. Their demand for excitement has often been satisfied in the intimate Bislett Stadium. With its six lane track and seating that comes right down to the track edge, the crowd can feel very close to the athletes. A marvellous atmosphere is soon generated and it is not surprising that many records have been broken there. In fact up until 1982, thirty-seven world records had been broken in the stadium. Perhaps the most exciting of these were the world record-breaking performances of Said Aouita, Sebastian Coe, Steve Ovett and Dave Moorcroft.

Bislett stadium at Oslo, Norway.

Crystal Palace

Crystal Palace is the national athletics arena of England, although in recent years it has been challenged by the Alexander Stadium in Birmingham. It was completed in 1968 and took over from the White City Stadium in the early 1970s as the national stadium and has a seating capacity of 17,000.

The track was relaid in 1983 and, according to the athletes, is much better for it. Its main international event of the year is the IAC Coca Cola Invitation meeting, which ends the British season. This meeting usually provides a host of exciting races as athletes try to finish the season with a good result.

Crystal Palace at London, England.

Meadowbank Stadium

The Meadowbank Stadium in Edinburgh became famous when it hosted the hugely successful 1970 Commonwealth Games. Few people who saw those Games will ever forget the tremendous atmosphere that prevailed throughout the two weeks.

Unfortunately, this atmosphere was not recreated when the Commonwealth Games were held there again in 1986. This was due to political boycotts from countries who resented Britain's links with South Africa.

Meadowbank Stadium at Edinburgh, Scotland.

Munich Stadium

When Munich was selected for the 1972 Olympic Games it constructed the most spectacular stadium and village the Games had ever seen, or indeed has seen since. The giant spider's web stadium was made of steel and Plexiglass, was larger than fourteen football pitches and cost $45 million to build. Four hundred companies were involved in its construction. At the opening ceremony 80,000 spectators filled the stadium, 7,131 athletes from 122 countries filled the centre of the stadium, 5,000 doves were released and 7,000 media people covered the event.

The stadium hosted many exciting races that year, but the 1972 Games were marred by the killing of eleven Israeli athletes by Palestinian terrorists. Perhaps because of this tragic incident, the stadium has not been used as much as it might have been for international athletics meetings.

Munich Stadium at Munich, Germany.

Los Angeles Coliseum

This beautiful stadium was built in 1923 and hosted both the 1932 and 1984 Olympic Games. Although it looks like an ancient amphitheatre it suffers from a very modern problem - smog. Before the 1984 Olympics, many of the distance runners were very worried about running in the heat and pollution of Los Angeles. These worries seemed to be justified as many athletes suffered badly in the conditions. However, there were many fine performances to compensate for this. These included some fine sprint performances which may have been helped by the new Rekortan synthetic track which was laid in 1983.

Los Angeles Coliseum at Los Angeles, USA.

The life of a professional athlete: Carl Lewis

Carl Lewis (USA), a legendary athlete, has been incredibly successful in both track and field events.

Carl Lewis (USA), is one of the greatest athletes there has ever been. He was born in 1962 into a very sporting family. His father, Bill, was a sprinter and long-jumper and his mother, Eve, was a hurdler in the 1951 Pan-American Games. He is 1.88m and weighs 78 Kg. As a ten-year-old boy, Carl Lewis met the great US athlete Jesse Owens. Jesse Owens had won four gold medals at the 1936 Berlin Olympics in the 100m, 200m, long-jump and relay. Owens had always been Lewis's biggest hero and his advice to the young Lewis was 'to have fun.' In the 1984 Los Angeles Olympics, Carl Lewis followed in the footsteps of Jesse Owens by also winning gold medals in the 100m, 200m, 4 × 100m relay and the long-jump

Carl Lewis's coach Tom Tellez, has devised a special programme of training for Lewis to reach his very best performance. Tellez worked out a percentage breakdown showing the important factors of Lewis's running:

- Reaction time out of blocks   1%
- Clearing the blocks   5%
- Efficient acceleration   64%
- Maintaining maximum speed   18%
- Limiting deceleration   12%

Carl Lewis's training is based on these figures. He starts his workout with a slow jog once around the track as preparation. He then concentrates most of all practising his acceleration. He goes through a series of distance sprints, trying harder and harder each time to regulate a constant acceleration. Endurance comes from stamina, and stamina comes with practise. But most of all Carl Lewis just likes 'to have fun'!

(Below left) Carl Lewis (USA) at home. One of Carl's favourite hobbies is cooking.

(Below centre) Carl Lewis (USA) is a very patriotic american.

(Below right) Carl Lewis (USA) likes to take part in the 4 × 100m relay team event, where four athletes compete together to win for their country. The smile on Carl's face shows his joy at winning the gold medal for the USA at the 1984 Los Angeles Olympics.

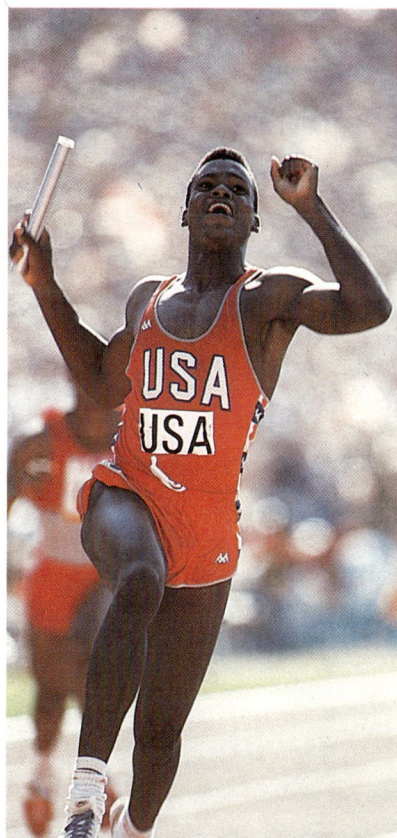

Great athletes

Jesse Owens (USA)

Jesse Owens became the hero of the 1936 Olympic Games when he won the 100m, 200m, the long jump and ran in the winning American 4 × 100m relay team. In doing so, he infuriated Hitler and made a nonsense of the Nazi propaganda that deemed blacks to be an inferior race. With his gentle manner and great modesty, this superb athlete won the hearts of thousands of German spectators and the acclaim of athletes and sports fans the world over. (For picture see page 7)

Ed Moses (USA)

Few people in the history of athletics have dominated an event as completely as Ed Moses did in the 400m hurdles. Between August 1977 and June 1987 Moses never lost a single race. His run came to an end on 4 June in Madrid when a fellow American, Danny Harris narrowly defeated the champion in a time of 47.56 seconds. Moses said after the race that he'd had an 'off-day' but that remains to be seen.

In 1976 when he was only twenty years old, he set a new world record of 47.64 seconds in winning the gold medal at the Montreal Olympics. He has since won every major championship title, holds the present world record of 47.02 seconds and, in the period up until 1983, held the nine fastest times ever recorded at the distance.

Ed Moses (USA) the champion 400m hurdler.

Emil Zatopek (Czechoslovakia)

At the 1948 Olympics in London Emil Zatopek won the 10,000m gold medal and was only just pushed into second place the next day in the 5,000m by Reiff of Belgium.

Four years later in 1952, at the Helsinki Olympic Games Zatopek established himself once again as one of history's great distance runners. At thirty years of age, he won the 10,000m gold medal and, in one of the most exciting races ever run, came back from being 150 metres behind on the last lap to take the gold in the 5,000m.

As if that wasn't enough two days later he went on to win the marathon, a distance he had never before attempted. In fact, he was so naive about the race that after a third of the race had gone he asked Peters of Great Britain and Janson of Sweden if they 'ought to be going faster'! He did, they didn't and Zatopek won another gold medal!

(Left) Emil Zatopek (Czechoslovakia) winning the 5,000m at the 1952 Helsinki Olympics.

Fanny Blankers-Koen (Holland)

In the 1936 Olympics, at the age of eighteen, Francis Koen, as she was then known, came sixth in the women's high jump. Disappointed with this result she resolved to dedicate herself to athletics and did so with startling results.

In 1948 at the age of thirty, she already held the world long and high jump records, but was advised not to compete in these events at the Olympics that year as she was pregnant. Many people also considered her to be too old to present a serious challenge, but in eight days she competed in, and won, eleven races. This brought her the 100m, 80m hurdles and 200m titles. In the women's 4 × 100m relay she brought the Dutch team back from fourth place to win the gold medal.

Fanny Blankers-Koen (Holland) at the front of the picture won three gold medals at the 1948 London Olympics.

Mary Decker-Slaney (USA)

This controversial figure was an international track star at the age of fourteen. When she was only fifteen she set a new world indoor 880 yds record, but her progress was marred by injury. She won the 1500m title at the 1983 World Championships and was favourite to win the gold medal at the Los Angeles Olympics in 1984. Unfortunately she was involved in an incident with Britain's Zola Budd which left her on the side of the track and out of the race. Her last chance to win an Olympic gold medal had perhaps gone forever.

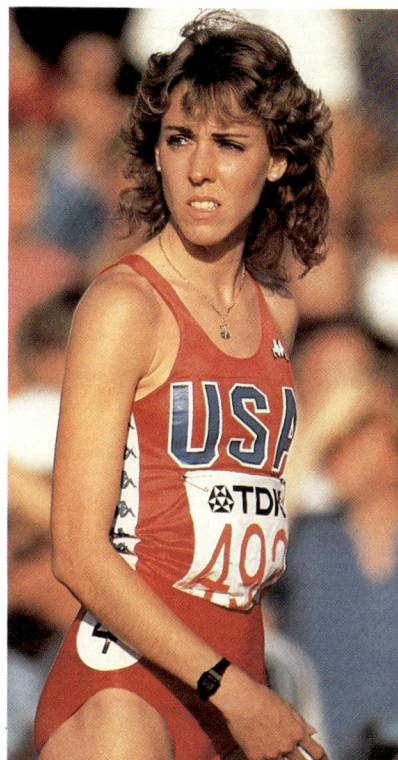

Mary Decker-Slaney (USA) champion at the 1500m.

Marita Koch (East German)

This superb athlete has been acclaimed as much for her versatility as her undoubted skill. In an incredibly competitive area of athletics she has managed to stay at the top in the 100m, 200m and 400m for many years. Whereas other athletes usually attempt longer distances as they get older, Koch moved down from the 400m to the 100m and 200m. She was the first woman to break 49 seconds for the 400m (48.94s in 1978) and twice broke the world 200m record in 1979 (22.02 seconds and 21.7 seconds).

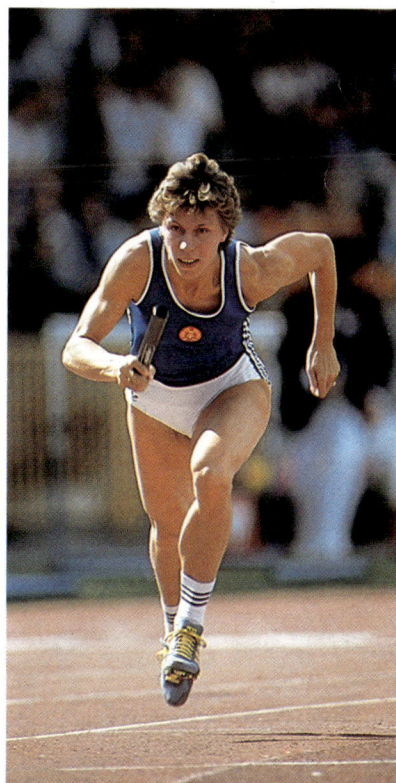

Marita Koch (East German) a versatile athlete has won 100m, 200m and 400m titles.

Glossary

Aerobic running – running at a pace where the body's demands for oxygen can be met.

Anaeorobic running – running at a pace where the body demands more oxygen than it can actually take in.

Break – when an athlete establishes a gap between himself and the rest of the runners.

Check marks – markers, such as pieces of tape, which act as a guide to an athlete's stride pattern.

Dip finish – a lunge from the waist upwards by an athlete to try and chest the tape first.

Fartlek – a form of training invented by a Swedish coach involving fast and slow running stretches.

Lactic acid – a substance produced in the joints of the body when it is subjected to hard, physical work.

Long-distance – generally considered to be all races above 3,000m.

Middle-distance – the 800m, 1500m and mile races.

Pack – the group of runners contesting a middle- or long-distance event.

Personal best – the best time, or distance, achieved by an athlete.

Split times – the times that an athlete performs for various stages of a race.

Sprints – the 100m, 200m and 400m races.

Staggered start – the placing of athletes at different stages of a bend at the start of a race, so that they all run the same distance.

Wall – the sudden tiredness that an athlete feels when his or her body starts to use its fat for energy, rather than the carbohydrates, which soon run out. Also describes the feeling an athlete experiences when he or she starts to run anaerobically.

Further reading

Better Athletics (Track) by John Heaton (Kay & Ward Ltd, 1973)

Athletics, Track Events by Tom McNab (Brockhampton Press Ltd, 1972)

The Olympics by Sebastian Coe with Nicholas Mason (Pavilion Books Ltd, 1984)

The Complete Book of Athletics by Tom McNab (Ward Books Ltd, 1980)

Enjoying Track and Field Sports by The Diagram Group (Paddington Press, 1979)

Useful addresses

Amateur Athletics Association
Francis House
Francis Street
London
SW1P 1DE

Australian Athletic Union
710–722 Mount Alexander Road
Moonee Ponds
Melbourne
Victoria
3039
Australia

New Zealand Amateur Athletic Association
P.O. Box 741
Wellington
New Zealand

Sports Council
16 Upper Woburn Place
London WC1

Canadian Track & Field Association
355 River Road
Tower B
Vanier City
Ottawa
Ontario KIL 8C1

Athletics Congress of USA
P.O. Box 120
Indianapolis
Indiana
46206–0120
USA

Index

figures in **bold** refer to illustrations